How You Can Achieve And Maintain Sales Success Today

In Sales Everything Counts

By: Richard J. Marcus

This publication is designed to provide accurate and authoritative information in regard to the subject matter covered. It is sold with the understanding that neither the author nor publisher is engaged in rendering legal, accounting or other professional service. If legal advice or other expert assistance is required, the services of a competent professional person should be sought.

ISBN-13: 978-1517411077
ISBN-10: 1517411076

Richard J. Marcus
Vue Coaching and Sales Training, LLC
3122-100 Fincher Farm Road, #214
Matthews, NC 28105

Website: http://www.vuecoaching.com

Phone: (704) 841-1036

Email: richardmarcus@vuecoaching.com

LinkedIn: https://www.linkedin.com/in/richardmarcus

Facebook: www.facebook.com/vuecoachingandsalestraining

Google+: https://plus.google.com/106204913240294472568/

Contents

Dedication

Before I tell you about me, let me tell you what I know about you. Sales Professionals, Entrepreneurs and Small Business Owners are the hardest working group of people in the world. You work in a tough profession characterized by constant change and tough competition. You are the lifeblood of your company and the generators of revenue for your businesses and family.

Selling is not going to get any easier, tough competition and a difficult market constantly challenge you, but you continue to sell, sell, sell. Day after day you face rejection, failure, and lies in order to make a living. I applaud you and certainly hope your family and employer appreciate your efforts and what you go through.

Sales people are "Action Takers," dealmakers and you make things happen. You take charge of all situations you can control and you skillfully managed through those you cannot control.

One more important fact I know about you- -you like to "Win" and you recognize in order to have a better life and sales success you have to get better. All top sales professionals commit to being life long learners of their profession.

Introduction

From an early age I recognized that the hallmark to developing character was helping others. I enjoyed helping my neighbors in Atlantic City do yard work and I never hesitated to help anyone in need if I could be of assistance. In college I volunteered at the YMCA and was also involved in the Big Brothers and Big Sisters organization.

After college I pursued my interest in helping others achieve their dreams by teaching business to juniors and seniors and co-coordinating the school's work/study program. Through this experience, my passion for helping others achieve their goals through both personal and professional development grew.

Now, 30 years later, I have had the opportunity to develop my skills as an Educator, Salesman, Trainer, Sales Manager and Marketing Manager. Through it all I have always felt privileged to be able to combine my enjoyment of helping others with my professional success.

Degrees, Certifications and Recognitions

- I have a BS degree in Business Education
- ICF approved Certified Professional Coach
- Certified Sales Trainer, Certified Sales Coach, Certified Interviewer
- Member of the *International Association of Coaching.*
- Recognized as the Top Sales Professional by NAPM
- Ranked in the Top 5% of Sales Professionals at a Global Fortune 500 Corporation

Training Credentials

- I have been an active participant in training from top companies such as Xerox, 3M and Arthur Anderson.
- I have developed training materials and delivered hundreds of sales seminars and presentations.
- In addition to recruiting and hiring staff, I have also trained and coached hundreds of sales people.
- Conducted hundreds of sales trainings and seminars.

Sales Credentials

- Over my 30 years in the business of sales, I have made thousands of cold calls, both over the phone and in person, and executed over 40,000 person-to-person sales calls.
- I have generated over $30 million in sales revenue.
- I have vast knowledge of 9 key B2B market Segments and years of experience working with B2C and B2G.

What Type of Company Seeks My Services?

I have worked with large corporations, small start up companies, entrepreneurs and small business ventures. This includes Wholesale Distributors, small manufacturers, privately held companies who sell in the B2B and B2G space and companies that deal with professional buyers and purchasing agents.

As an entrepreneur myself, I know what it takes to lead other start-ups and small businesses so that they reach their sales goals. If you need a coach to help you and your team increase sales, let me show you strategies that will work for your business.

How I Work

I am a task-oriented individual and proceed with a logical, careful pace to ensure that every project is completed well and on-time. I thoroughly think through all angles of a problem and deliberately choose precise and clear words to limit misinformation or misunderstandings.

My work experience has given me the confidence to know that I can help businesses increase sales and productivity.

What I Can Do For Your Business

I can do for your business, what I have done for hundreds of others. My affordable coaching will help you obtain more prospects, increase your margins and commissions, and get more phone calls returned. Through my coaching you will develop more confidence, motivation and focus.

YOU GET 5 BIG BENEFITS FROM WORKING WITH ME!

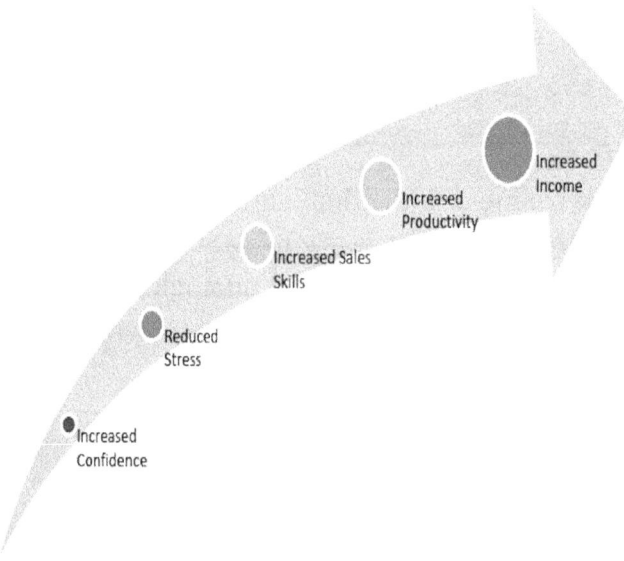

Increased Income

Increased Productivity

Increased Sales Skills

Reduced Stress

Increased Confidence

Testimonials

Below are a few comments from clients who have used my services and have been able to obtain their desired results.

E.S., Retired Lt. Col USMC
"I have observed many individuals in the business world, but it does renew my confidence in the process to see such a leader as Richard."

J.F., VP Marketing, Wholesale Distribution Corp.
"Richard brings a strong understanding of business principles and professionalism to any organization he is associated with."

B.L., Managing Partner, Network Marketing Corp.
"Richard has been a great coach & role model."

Z.M., Team Leader, National Paper Mfg.
"I am a manager and I utilize some of the skills Richard taught me. Richard was very patient and a pleasure to work with."

D.N., Purchasing Manager, Jan-San Supply Company
"Richard is very upbeat and positive. He was always there for our company and I will use his services again."

J.B., National Industrial Sales Rep. *"Richard has lots of knowledge and experience. I am pleased to recommend him."*

10 B2B Sales Skills Every Professional Sales Person Must Have

There are dozens of selling skills that B2B Sales Professionals should possess. I've tried to condense the list down to what are the most important 10 skills every B2B Sales Professional must be proficient at in order to achieve and maintain sales success today.

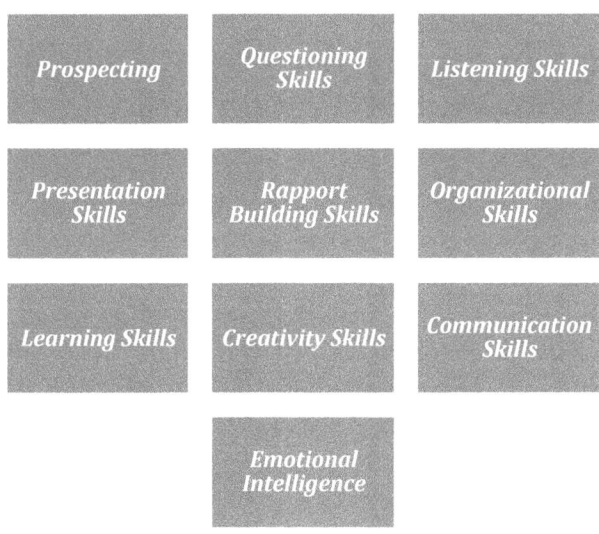

"You Don't Have To Sell Alone. Help Is Available"

Sales Tips

12 Tough Challenges B2B Sales Professionals Face Today

In the competitive, tough and demanding world of B2B Sales, building a solid foundation of sales skills, people skills and the ability to stay motivated and focused will carry you far in this sales profession. My goal as a Sales Coach and Trainer is to assist sales professionals on their journey to sell at an elite level. Listed below are 12 of the most prevalent challenges you will face as you achieve and maintain sales success today.

➤ *Inability to Get Through To Key Decision Makers!*

Solution: Connect first – approach without trying to sell. Offer something of value. Ask for advice on a key industry matter. Get a referral. Recognize a C-Level Strategy would be very different from a strategy to reach a lower level decision maker.

➤ *Competing Is Tough ---Too Many Competitors!*

Solution: You cannot reduce the number of competitors in your market, but you can outsell them by being Sales Distinctive. There are many ways, I'm going to give you a couple: First I want you to repeat the following statement several times, *"In Sales Everything Counts."* As you embrace this thought in your mind you will look for ways to become more creative.

One way to outsell many competitors is to be seen as a credible professional. Use professional literature, get a testimonial and write an article about a subject that is important to your prospects. Here is one more option, know your competition like you know the back of your hand. Why do prospects/customers like them? Why do they win or lose business? Use a Competitive Points Summary to compare you and your company. Contact me for a customized (CPS)

➢ *Dealing with Budget Cutbacks - -Bad Economy!*

Solution: Whether you sell a service or a product, offering a "cost savings" is a sure way to get your prospects attention. Do you have examples of how you were able to lower cost? Don't cut your prices, but do offer lower cost products if you have them. Can you offer information or be a resource to your prospects/customers on other goods and services that can help them?

Stay focused on your sales and income goals and don't get distracted with all the bad news. Keep prospecting because companies are always buying.

➢ *Finding More Qualified Leads!*

Solution: Your Marketing Dept. can help if you have one. They have money set aside for lead generation, be sure you're taking advantage of this resource. Here are a few more options: Chamber of Commerce membership, personal networking and Social Media. Your state, local and county governments all have data on the largest area employers.

Paid and unpaid advertising produces leads as well as participating with targeted non-profits.

➢ *Lack of Skill to Build Trust & Credibility With Prospects!*

Solution: My number one biased answer, hire a Sales Coach we solve this problem. Additionally there are plenty of books, CD's and webinars on how to develop this skill. Furthermore trust and credibility building is a process. During initial contact you absolutely must ask high value questions focused on prospect needs and their situation and listen to the answers. Believe me when you master asking high value questions and listening you are on your way to sales success. A good habit to develop is to ask permission to ask questions.

Here is an example of a high value question; Mr. Property Mgr. Class A Office Building Managers tell us they are constantly challenged to reduce cost and maintain quality while decreasing tenant complaints. Are these issues you are currently facing?

This question establishes your knowledge of the office building business and will earn you the right to continue a conversation.

➢ *Difficulty Handling Objections!*

Solution: To respond to an objection properly first make sure it's a real objection. Identify 3 objections you generally encounter and write down 2-3 responses to each one. I want you to take your time while doing this and be sure to practice your responses so they sound natural when you speak. You can feel confident knowing that you have prepared for the toughest objections.

➢ *Technical Skills & People Skills Are Out Of Balance!*

Solution: Being proficient in spreadsheets, math and technology is important. Let me be clear Sales is a people business and soft skills are even more important. This is how Wikipedia defines soft skills (I call them people skills):

Soft skills is a term often associated with a person's "EQ" (Emotional Intelligence Quotient), the cluster of personality traits, social graces, communication, language, personal habits, interpersonal skills, managing people, leadership, etc. that characterize relationships with other people. Soft skills contrast to hard skills, which are generally easily quantifiable and measurable (e.g. software knowledge, basic plumbing skills).

A person's soft skill EQ is an important part of their individual contribution to the success of an organization. Particularly those organizations dealing with customers face-to-face are generally more successful, if they train their staff to use these skills. Screening or training for personal habits or traits such as dependability and conscientiousness can yield significant return on investment for an organization. For this reason, soft skills are increasingly sought out by employers in addition to standard qualifications.

➤ *Prospecting Skills Not Up To Date!*

Solution: This is closely related to #4 above and is an absolute needed skill in order to survive and thrive in sales. Most sales people hate this part of sales. You probably already have your own style, so try incorporating these tips into your methodology. Here's what I want you to do right now, think about the last 3 voice mail messages you left for a prospect. Ok, now go leave each of those messages on your own voice mail. Listen and make any changes - if you were a prospect would you want to listen to these prospecting messages? How many times did you use the word "I" or our company? Remember it's not about you.

Alright let's do 1 more; whether it's voice mail, email or in person always focus on what's important to the prospect/customer. What one or two issues have you identified through your research that your target market needs help or answers? These issues should be the focus of all your communications with these prospects. One note of caution before I move on, don't try and close people just because you know of their issues or they have stated their issues. Part of the prospecting process is you determining if they want to take action to resolve their issues.

➢ Inability to Be Sales Distinctive!

Solution: You can be distinctive professionally and personally. Here are a few suggestions: instead of just voice mails, how about using video emails? Instead of email how about hand written letters and notes? What if you noticed all your competitors don't wear suit Jackets or ties etc., you should start wearing suits. Do you have a personal website? How about buying a domain name for your top 3 customers? As you review the above list you will start thinking how creative you could be and the fun you will have as you begin your journey of "Sales Distinctiveness."

➤ Not Planning Sales Strategy & Setting Goals!

Solution: There are many tools (fill in the blank type) available to walk you through this process. You are aware of the importance of goal setting and developing a strategy. Use any of these tools to get started: your CRM system, 30-60-90 Day Plan, or software available to purchase. If you don't have a sales manager to assist you, your measurable goals might be based on future planned purchases.

How much do you need to increase your commissions to buy a new car, house down payment or vacation? As you plan and strategize make sure to write your goals down, have a date/timetable to complete, have a system in place to measure your progress. Whether you're a business owner or and individual professional the process is the same.

➢ Lack of Resources!

Solution: Dealing with this challenge is always tough. You need resources to generate sales and income; and you need sales to generate the resources. Individuals and small businesses face this same challenge. Some options are to borrow money for marketing, training and advertising. Go bare bones and generate sales revenue then set a percentage aside, or you can join Trade & Barter Associations which eliminates the need for cash. With bartering, members literally trade with other members to get the services/products they need for their businesses.

➢ Not Differentiating Between Sales & Marketing!

Solution: Let's talk about why you need to know the difference …many sales people and small business owners I talk to confuse the Sales and Marketing functions. They both have the same goal, which is to find and keep customers. Functionally the sales part is tactical and the marketing part is more strategic. Today we live in a knowledge/information based economy and consumers can readily access information on your products/services and those of your competitors almost instantaneously. Because of these dynamics Marketing has become especially important.

Marketing are those activities that generate leads, create desire and gain positive attention for you or your business. Selling is the process involving all activities that gain commitments and close the sale. As you look at your business or your sales performance determine which area could use some tweaking and call an expert.

Common Sales Mistakes You Can Stop Today

Selling directly to consumers is dramatically different than selling to other businesses! Sooner or later Sales Professionals will realize that, *In Sales Everything Counts*!

B2B customers are highly informed and much more sophisticated than consumers because their purchases are usually part of a complex supply chain, higher in dollar volume and represent a unique business model. Selling B2B requires the sales professional to understand not just products, people and best business practices but industries, trends, organization, and multifaceted internal business processes.

Following are some common actions to put on your "don't do" list. I must admit I have made some of these mistakes, but you don't have to. These are not in any particular order. Here is to your continued sales success!

1) **Not being an active listener**. What exactly is "Active Listening"?

The act of mindfully hearing and attempting to comprehend the meaning of words and body language spoken by a prospect/customer in a conversation. Active listening is an important business communication skill, and it can involve making sounds that indicate attentiveness, as well as the listener giving feedback in the form of a paraphrased rendition of what has been said by the other party for their confirmation. It's important to focus on what is being said and not what your response will be. Maintain eye contact and be sure to pause before speaking. Active listening is a great way to build trust and develop rapport.

Here are a couple of things you can say to demonstrate **Active Listening**:

    a) It seems to me that you feel....
    b) I really hear you saying....

2) **Not planning the sales call**.

This is a really critical area that often sets the stage for the entire interaction. Have clear objectives of what you want to accomplish; you'll want to determine if this account is worth your time, identify key decision makers, compile a list of potential questions to ask, familiarize yourself with any burning issues in this industry and who are this prospects key competitors. Lastly gain an understanding of how this company buys what you are selling so you can adjust your sales activities to match.

3) **Not taking notes**.

This is a part of active listening and provides visual proof you're listening. Additional benefits gained from taking notes:
- You capture important information,
- It makes you look professional,

- It makes the prospect feel important,
- Notes spark more ideas,
- It improves your memory and
- Gives the prospect confidence their important needs are captured.

4) **Not following up**.

It's your responsibility to get commitments for and follow up appointments. ***Make sure you have a compelling reason to initiate any follow up actions***. Having a strategy to keep momentum and sales velocity is a must. Be sensitive to the timing and how often you follow up. There is a delicate balance between persistence and being perceived as an arrogant pest. Whether it's mailing analysis, testimonials, making phone calls, sending samples, price quotes, MSDS Sheets or relevant articles. Emails and voice mails also must be used strategically. Follow up is also holding the prospect accountable for their commitments.

5) **Not planning the day efficiently**.

Wake up every morning with 3 to 5 objectives on your To-Do list. Prioritize your activities so the most impactful and important things get taken care of immediately. Without daily goals it's easy to fall into a sales rut. Allow enough time between appointments so you're not stressed. Have a set time to check your email, and to prioritize which phone calls to return or initiate.

6) **Not looking your best**.

Believe it or not prospects and customers do judge a book by its cover. Your personal appearance is your cover. *In Sales Everything Counts*. Shoes should be shined, pants/shirt ironed. Whatever the dress code is for our industry, exceed it. Ladies you should be appropriately dressed for business, not nightclubs.

Now I know some of you reading this are saying, "Really Richard? Do you really have to talk about this?" The answer is yes. You'd be surprised by the number of high heels, big earring, over bearing perfume, low cut blouses, and inappropriate make up I've seen on sales calls. Your personal appearance is part of establishing your credibility and personal brand. Don't give prospects any reason not to talk to you.

7) **Not asking for the sale**.

After the demos, trials, cost savings analysis, questions answered and proposals are submitted, now it's time to ask for the business. You have earned the right to ask for the business. Be confident because this is what all the time you've invested has been leading up to. Some sales people let fear of "No" paralyze them, but if you covered all-important items in the prospects buying process, they expect you to ask for the business. Here are some examples of powerful ways to ask for the business:

a) Mr. Prospect have we met all your requirements and specifications in a professional manner? If they answer yes, then your response is, "When can I pick up the Purchase Order?"

b) Ms. Prospect do you have any questions or concerns I have not covered so far? If the answer is no, you can ask, "How would you like to proceed?"

c) Mr. Prospect we have spent a lot of time developing this program together. How do you feel about what we have accomplished so far? If there are no issues, ask for the requisition.

In professional selling, success belongs to the "*Askers*," those that ask for the business at the right time after the right actions have been taken. Feel free to modify these for your specific industry.

8) **Not knowing when to stop talking**.

Harvard University did a study on why people talk too much and concluded it makes us feel good. However, one of the most common complaints from prospects about sales people is that they talk too much. Conversational narcissism can hurt your sales efforts, building rapport and gaining prospect confidence in you.

A few other reasons sales people talk too much is anxiety, lack of preparation, ego and lack of confidence. Additionally, poor training causes sales people to talk too much. Some companies have structured sales programs, which encourage the sales people to talk too much about their products, services and strategies. Staying focused on the prospect will help you listen more and talk less.

9) **Not keeping up-to-date**.

You are probably aware now of the importance of keeping your sales skills "up to date" and the enormous benefits of constant learning. Imagine how confident you'll feel when you read articles about sales best practices, attend a sales seminar/webinar or practice with your peers. This is one way to prove you are a sales professional.

Today prospects view all sellers the same. If you want to differentiate yourself, "keeping up to date" is your ticket. How would it feel if you were able to get your prospects to view you as credible? How would it feel if you were able to get your prospects to say you understand my needs? This is what keeping up-to-date will do for you.

10) **Not hiring a sales coach with a solid track record to help you**. ☺

In the next section I will discuss what to look for when hiring a sales coach.

"I choose to make a positive impact on people's lives."
–   Richard Marcus

Hiring a Sales Coach

If your sales are not what you would like them to be, or if you would just like to take your business to the next level, hiring a sales coach is something to consider.

10 Reasons to Have a Sales Coach

1) *You have other people depending on your success.*

2) *You want to increase your earned commissions.*

3) *You want to learn how to ask better questions.*

4) *You want objective feedback on your sales process.*

5) *You are a small business that cannot afford a full-time sales manager.*

6) *You have committed to improve yourself by 1% but are not sure how to get that result.*

7) *You want to improve your communication process skills.*

8) *You want to learn how to make yourself distinctive.*

9) *You want another source of creative, proven ideas.*

10) *You realize the sales process is complicated and that it is better to not go it alone.*

If any of these resonate with you, take the time to explore hiring a sales coach. Just like in sports, having the right coach to help you refine your game plan can make all the difference between having a winning or losing season.

Top 10 Questions to Ask Before Hiring a Sales Coach

The process of hiring a sales coach should not be taken lightly since the right coach can significantly increase your business' revenue and the wrong coach could do just the opposite.

There are many sales coaches and companies offering quick and unbelievable results. This can make it difficult to know where to start or what to look for when hiring a coach.

Here are my top 10 questions to ask before you hire a sales coach so you can reach your full sales potential. Along with each question is MY answer to the question. This will enable you to compare between my service and others that you may be considering.

1) *What is your personal track record of success in sales*?

I have 25 + years of successful sales, sales management, training and marketing experience for two Fortune 500 Companies and I generated millions in Sales Revenue. I know what it takes to become a top sales professional. I was ranked in the top 5% among my peers and have received numerous sales awards.

Ask potential coaches: have you ever been a successful 100% commission salesman?

Many sales coaches do not have the credentials of being a top performer in a large organization multiple times. Others do not have extensive experience building, developing and managing sales forces.

But what if those are your goals? See the concern? If they have not walked the walk, and proven they know what it takes to achieve great sales results, how can you expect them to know what it takes to achieve extraordinary results?

Now, it can be hard to find a sales coach's past sales performance on his or her website or on LinkedIn, so be sure to ask or do your own online research and find out.

To get where you want to go, you need a coach that has already been there.

2) *Will you customize your sales coaching programs around my particular needs and goals?*

Many sales coaching programs simply place all individuals and businesses into the exact same sales coaching process. In effect, each business or individual is taught in a training format that starts with certain skills or techniques and moves on to the next set of techniques. They do not take into consideration the immediate challenges at hand, nor do they focus on customizing the program around the strengths of the individual or organization, while identifying and addressing weaknesses.

Before you hire a sales coach, ask how they customize their sales coaching program. If they don't have some good examples to share, run fast, or face receiving cookie-cutter coaching which will greatly impede your results.

3) *What is your general sales philosophy?*

Sales coaches often have a very traditional perspective when it comes to sales and selling. This results in the coach teaching you to persuade, push, be very aggressive, and to forcefully change the mind of others. This will make both you and the prospective client feel uncomfortable. This will automatically lead to lost sales.

Many of the old persuasive selling techniques really are a thing of the past. They don't work. Yet, many sales coaches are still teaching the same stuff. If you want to reach your sales potential then you need a sales coach who understands how to create a genuine, natural, customized sales philosophy for each individual they coach. If they don't, watch out.

4) *Do you have professional coaching training and sales training certifications?*

You may find a sales coach who has a respectful sales background like me. But, in many cases they'll have very little, if any professional coaching training or professional sales training. There is a big difference between calling oneself a coach, and having many hours of hours of face-to-face coaching training. What professional credentials and certifications have you obtained?

If they do not have this training, you may not receive all the support you need around motivation, focus, changing your mind set, accountability, and being able to support you towards success. If you hire a sales coach who does not have professional training, do not expect the same results. You will not be supported holistically around all the intangibles that help people reach extraordinary results.

5) *Do you offer monthly programs?*

Many sales coaching programs involve a 6-month or longer commitment or a large upfront investment just to get started. Be careful, because if you don't see the results you want with your sales coach, you are stuck. Look for a coach who offers flexibility. Including, month-to-month programs or packages that enable you to minimize your upfront risk as you initiate your partnership with the sales coach.

When working with a top-level expert sales coach, you should quickly see results. Then you make the decision to invest in the coaching, versus being trapped in a long-term agreement with a coach who is not an ideal fit for you.

6) *What experience do you have managing or leading a sales force?*

Often a sales coach may have experience selling, but they will have little or no experience actually managing, developing and leading sales teams. If you are a business owner who is focused on building and developing your sale team, then you need a sales coach who has something of value to offer.

7) *Why did you become a sales coach and sales trainer?*

Find out if the sales coach made the conscious choice to become a coach for the right reasons, or if they burned out of corporate America or fell into the position as a backup because they lost a job. You want a coach who loves coaching, sales, and changing lives. Look for a coach with whom you an connect.

Look for a sales coach who truly cares about your success and loves the work he or she does. If you do not sense a great deal of passion in their voice when they describe how they became a sales coach, talk to another coach.

8) *How else can you support me to achieve my goals?*

The sales coach you are thinking about hiring may know how to sell, but does this sales coach lack the necessary skills to provide the support you need when it comes to mindset, motivation, focus, productivity, effectiveness, and discipline. Teaching and sharing new skills is just one small piece of effective sales coaching. When an expert sales coach can support a client with all the intangibles, far greater results are possible. Pay attention to how they answer this question and ask for examples.

9) *Can you show me new and innovative ways to increase my business?*

If the sales coach is not aware of how to use social media, blogs, website marketing, SEO, effective article writing, article marketing, LinkedIn, Twitter, and other similar tools to grow their own business, how can they help you to grow yours?

Technology is always changing and there are ways to use it to increase your sales results. Find a sales coach who is using these tools on a daily basis to grow their sales coaching business. Find a sales coach who can show you how to generate leads, contact new prospects and network effectively in the modern era of sales. If they don't use these tools, keep on looking.

10) *Do you have a coach?*

After a 25+ year successful career with two Fortune 500 companies I still work with a coach and have a support network. I get a tremendous amount out of it and I am convinced of the value of coaching. How can you be a coach, but say you don't need a coach yourself?

Even the most successful people in the world have coaches to stay on top and reach even higher levels of success. As soon as you stop learning, growing, improving and developing, what kind of an example are you showing for your own clients? Find a sales coach who has a coach, believes in coaching, uses coaching to continue to become a better coach, a better entrepreneur, and a better person.

Find someone who inspires you to do more and doesn't just coach you, but leads by example. If they don't have a coach, just ask them why. This is an important question to ask and I'm guessing you will decide to move on pretty fast after they say they don't need a coach or don't have one.

Find a sales coach who is right for you by asking these questions. Look for a Sales Coach and a certified Sales Trainer who truly cares about you and your success. Make sure the sales coach you select takes the time to get to know you, your sales goals and challenges. Follow these tips and you will ensure you partner up with the right sales coach for you to achieve amazing sales results.

Next Steps

When you are ready to take your sales to the next level, I am currently offering two specials:

1) "Personalized Sales Check Up"

2) LinkedIn Profile Makeover

Contact me today to schedule a consultation.

Richard J. Marcus
Vue Coaching and Sales Training, LLC
3122-100 Fincher Farm Road, #214
Matthews, NC 28105

Website: http://www.vuecoaching.com

Phone: (704) 841-1036

Email: richardmarcus@vuecoaching.com

LinkedIn: https://www.linkedin.com/in/richardmarcus

Facebook: www.facebook.com/vuecoachingandsalestraining

Google+: https://plus.google.com/106204913240294472568/